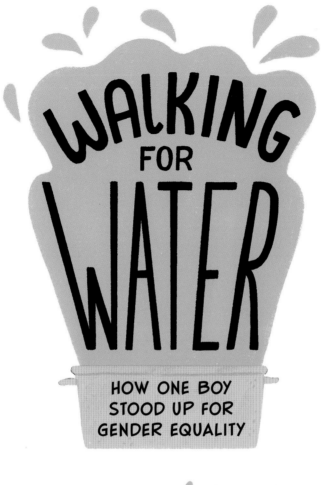

WALKING FOR WATER

HOW ONE BOY STOOD UP FOR GENDER EQUALITY

Susan Hughes  Nicole Miles

CitizenKid™

A collection of books that inform children about the world
and inspire them to be better global citizens

Kids Can Press

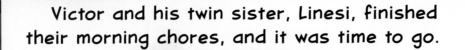

Victor and his twin sister, Linesi, finished their morning chores, and it was time to go.

Bye, Mama!

Tionana, Mama!

Ndimakukondani!

How embarrassing! thought Victor. Mama didn't always need to remind them — and all the neighbors — that she loved him and his sister. She'd already kissed them each a dozen times that morning!

Race you!

Victor and Linesi ran all the way to the *kachere* tree.

3

At the tree, Linesi and her friend Enifa knocked their water buckets together in greeting and headed off to the riverbed.

Victor felt a weird tug at his heart. It still felt strange to go to school without his sister.

Come on, tortoise!

But then, Enifa's brother, Chikondi, yelled to Victor, who hurried to catch up, shrugging the feeling away.

Victor was glad when math time was over. Nothing could make him like doing calculations. But Victor *did* like his new teacher.

Mr. Tambala let the class practice their vocabulary words by using them in silly sentences.

The space alien loved the taste of the roasted potato.

The snake slid down the slippery slide.

And now Mr. Tambala was using funny voices as he read aloud to the class, something their old teacher never did.

Victor turned to share a laugh with Linesi ...

... But, that's right. She wasn't there.

Everyone in the village needed water for drinking, cooking and washing, but there wasn't a well. The women and older girls fetched the water for their families from the river. That's how it had always been.

So when Victor and his sister had turned eight a few weeks ago, just at the start of the school year, Linesi began the daily walks for water, giving Mama more time for the farming.

Watching Linesi strut around like she was all grown up, Victor had almost wished *he* got to collect the water. But not anymore. Every day now, Linesi was missing school to collect water. Five walks to the river and five walks home.

Later in the afternoon, Mr. Tambala surprised the class with something new again. Something their old teacher had never talked to them about.

Equality means everyone — boys *and* girls — has the same rights. Boys and girls should also have the same opportunities.

Of course we are!

We'll be talking more about this in the days to come, but first, some homework. Look at your own lives. Think about whether boys and girls are treated equally.

And school was over for the day. Victor stopped and looked. All the girls in his class headed home to do chores, but the boys ...

When Victor got home from playing, his sister was there, helping Mama prepare the evening meal.

And after they ate, Linesi cleaned up while he did homework. Tonight, that meant thinking about whether he and Linesi had equal opportunities.

Well, I have lots of choices ... I want a family of my own one day, but first, I want to finish school.

I could try to get a job here or in town. I could own a shop or drive a truck. Maybe I could be a teacher or a lawyer.

But Linesi? Already, she isn't going to school anymore.

Later that evening, Victor tried to show Linesi what she'd missed in school that day.

But he couldn't explain math in the clear way Mr. Tambala did.

And the next night, Linesi was too tired to even try to learn. Victor found himself thinking more about equality.

In the morning, after Victor and Linesi raced each other to the *kachere* tree, Victor watched Linesi head off to the river.

This *wasn't* equality.

Definitely not. Linesi should get to keep learning and maybe become a teacher or a lawyer, too, if she wanted.

So that evening, Victor gathered his family.

I have a plan.

Victor, Linesi and Mama talked for a long time. And by the end of the evening, they had all agreed to try Victor's idea.

The next morning, the twins met their friends at the *kachere* tree as usual. But this time, it was Linesi who headed down the path to school with Chikondi.

Victor felt a different kind of tug at his heart. Now, it felt strange to see his sister going to school without *him*.

Well, come on, tortoise!

Victor grinned and joined the line of women and girls walking to the river.

That day, it was Victor who walked back and forth to the river five times.

The walk was long, and the bucket was heavy. He got tired. And bored. He even practiced math calculations in his head to pass the time.

But he was proud to be helping his family. And happy his sister was at school.

Then the next day, it was Linesi's turn to walk for water and Victor's turn to go to school.

And the day after that, they switched again ...

and again ...

and again.

Their evenings were different now, too.

One night, Victor would help Linesi keep up with the work she missed.

The next night, Linesi helped Victor with his.

As well, just as Mr. Tambala
had promised, the class continued
their talks about equality.

And so, the very next week, there was another change. When the twins arrived at the *kachere* tree, they saw Chikondi, not Enifa, holding a water bucket!

So many changes! And more coming—maybe Mr. Tambala giving extra classes, maybe a village well, but for sure, more changes to bring equality to boys and girls in the village. Victor was sure because he was determined to help make them happen.

But that was for later. Right now, it was time to run—all the way to the *kachere* tree!

29

Author's Note

Walking for Water is set in a small village in Malawi, a country in the southeastern part of the continent of Africa. Because Malawians are known for their kindness and friendliness, the country is sometimes called "the warm heart of Africa."

Malawi has a large population for its small size, with most of the people living in rural areas and in poverty. And although there is plenty of water in Malawi — it has one of the world's largest freshwater lakes — much of it is not safe to drink. Most of the people in rural areas have difficulty accessing any water sources at all, safe or not!

This lack of access to clean water often means hours of walking back and forth from wells, streams or rivers every day. Traditionally, girls and women in Malawi take on this time-consuming, physically demanding task. (You can imagine how this can make many girls so exhausted that they end up quitting school.)

In Malawi, as in many other places in the world, girls do not enjoy all the rights and opportunities boys do. Just as you read in *Walking for Water*, girls are given many of the household chores while the boys are allowed time to play and do homework. More time for their studies means boys often do better in school, which gives them even more advantages than girls. Plus, many girls are forced to marry at a young age. And when they do, they usually drop out of school, reducing their chances of earning a good income.

But things are beginning to change. For example, in 2017, Malawi raised the minimum age of marriage from 15 to 18. And by 2018, 80 percent of the country's population had access to an improved source of drinking water. Individual Malawians also continue taking action for change.

In fact, the story in *Walking for Water* was inspired by the recent experience of a thoughtful and fair-minded 13-year-old Malawian boy. After learning about gender equality at school, he realized there was inequality in his own community and in his own family. He wanted to do something about it. So he began walking for water. He knew it would give his mother and sister more time to do other important things, such as farm for food, go back to school and enjoy family life! And as a bonus, he became a role model for the other boys and for everyone in the village.

You can learn more about issues of water scarcity and gender inequality in Malawi and other countries by reading about or contacting the following organizations:

Charity: Water
This group works with local organizations in countries around the world to fund clean water projects.
www.charitywater.org

Girls Empowerment Network Malawi
This rights organization supports girls and young women in Malawi who are fighting for gender equality in health, education and economic opportunities, as well as for a just society.
www.genetmalawi.org

The Hunger Project – Malawi
This organization helps communities struggling to overcome hunger and poverty join together when advocating to their local government for funds and support.
www.thp.org/what-we-do/where-we-work/africa/malawi/

World Vision – Malawi
This humanitarian group works to end poverty and injustice in Malawi and improve the lives of its roughly four million children.
www.wvi.org/malawi

Words to Know

These words are in Chichewa, one of several languages spoken in Malawi.

kachere (ka-CHE-rey)
a type of wild fig tree; in Malawi, it is sometimes seen as a symbol of unity for the community.

ndimakukondani (nedee-ma-ku-ko-N'DA-nee)
"I love you."

tionana (tee-o-NA-na)
"See you later."

tsiku labwino (tsi-koo la-BWI-no)
"Have a good day" or "Good day."

To the real Victor, with great admiration — S.H.
For Sage, Chiji, Obi, Ozi, Renzo and Amara.
Learn and love and live with all your heart. — N.M.

Thank you to Malawian freelance columnist Veronica Maele for her generosity in reviewing this story in all its many drafts and to Dr. Lucinda Manda-Taylor of the University of Malawi for consulting on the art. Thanks also go to Sam Mchombo, an associate professor in the Department of African American Studies at the University of California, Berkeley, who, with his expertise in linguistics and the Chichewa language, consulted on the pronunciation guide. And another thank you to journalist Tyler Riewer for writing the photo essay that inspired this project and for providing answers to my many questions. — S.H.

Text © 2021 Susan Hughes
Illustrations © 2021 Nicole Miles

Published in Canada and the U.S. by Kids Can Press Ltd.
25 Dockside Drive, Toronto, ON M5A 0B5

Kids Can Press is a Corus Entertainment Inc. company

www.kidscanpress.com

The artwork in this book was rendered in Photoshop and Procreate.
The text is set in Blambot FX Pro Light.

Edited by Stacey Roderick and Kathleen Keenan
Designed by Marie Bartholomew

Printed and bound in Malaysia in 10/2020 by Tien Wah Press (Pte) Ltd.

CM 21 0 9 8 7 6 5 4 3 2 1

FSC
www.fsc.org
MIX
Paper from
responsible sources
FSC® C012700

LIBRARY AND ARCHIVES CANADA CATALOGUING IN PUBLICATION

Title: Walking for water : how one boy stood up for gender equality /
written by Susan Hughes ; illustrated by Nicole Miles.
Names: Hughes, Susan, 1960- author. | Miles, Nicole, illustrator.
Series: CitizenKid.
Description: Series statement: CitizenKid
Identifiers: Canadiana 20200226770 | ISBN 9781525302497 (hardcover)
Classification: LCC PS8565.U42 W35 2021 | DDC jC813/.6 — dc23

Kids Can Press gratefully acknowledges that the land on which our office is located
is the traditional territory of many nations, including the Mississaugas of the Credit, the Anishnabeg,
the Chippewa, the Haudenosaunee and the Wendat peoples, and is now home to many diverse
First Nations, Inuit and Métis peoples.

We thank the Government of Ontario, through Ontario Creates; the Ontario Arts Council;
the Canada Council for the Arts; and the Government of Canada
for supporting our publishing activity.